jambo means hello

jambo means hello

SWAHILI ALPHABET BOOK

by Muriel Feelings · pictures by Tom Feelings

THE DIAL PRESS · NEW YORK

Composition by The Composing Room, Inc.
Printed by Connecticut Printers, Inc.
Bound by Economy Bookbinding Corporation
Designed by Atha Tehon

To my other family,
the Apondos

Tutaonana

the continent of Africa,
showing countries where
Swahili is spoken

NILE

RIVER

SOMALIA

CONGO

ZAIRE

UGANDA KENYA

Kampala ★

★ Mogadishu

RWANDA

★ Kigali

★ Nairobi

Bujumbura ★

BURUNDI

+ MT. KILIMANJARO

Brazzaville ★

★ Kinshasa

TANZANIA

★ Dar es Salaam

Z A M B I A

MALAWI

Lusaka ★

Zomba ★

MOZAMBIQUE

MALAGASY REPUBLIC

★ Tananarive

★ Lourenço Marques

introduction

The purpose of this book is to introduce the reader to Swahili words. Learning a language opens up many things to us. With new words come new ideas and an understanding of the people and environment which created the language.

Swahili is spoken across more of Africa than any other language. It is the language of about 45 million people in eastern Africa, in all or parts of the countries of Kenya, Uganda, the People's Republic of the Congo (Brazzaville), Zaire, Somalia, Tanzania, Rwanda, Burundi, Zambia, Malawi, Mozambique, and the Malagasy Republic. Swahili varies in dialect from one area to another: that spoken on the coast of East Africa from that of the interior, that of Uganda from the Congo and other countries. In the same way, the Spanish language differs in dialect in the various provinces of Spain and in South America and the Caribbean Isles. But the important thing is that the peoples of the various East African countries can make themselves understood to one another despite these small differences. Because Swahili is spoken across such a vast area of the African continent, it could one day serve as the continental language.

For purposes of simplicity I have referred to the language as *Swahili,* but properly called it is *Kiswahili.* The *Ki* prefix denotes the actual language as opposed to the people who speak the language.

It should be noted that there are no *Q* or *X* sounds in Swahili; hence there are only twenty-four letters in the alphabet. The sound of the letter *G* is hard as in *give,* and the *R* is like the Spanish *R,* made by rolling the tongue.

There is a Swahili proverb that says: *Haba na haba hujaza kibaba:*

Little by little fills the measure. It is hoped that through this introduction to Swahili, children of African ancestry will seek to learn more "little by little," through available books, people, and travel.

Muriel Feelings

jambo means hello

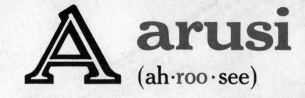

A arusi
(ah·roo·see)

is a wedding

When two people marry, it is an important event for their village as well as for their families. It is celebrated with drumming, dancing, and much food for all.

B baba means father
(bah·bah)

Parents teach their children the things they will need to know when they are grown. The father teaches his sons to build the home and to make tools.

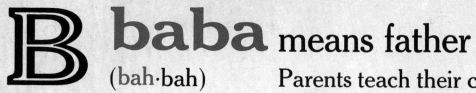

C chakula is food

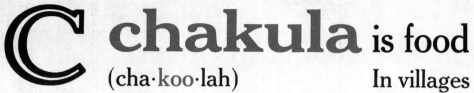

(cha·koo·lah)

In villages the people grow most of their food. Together many families raise crops like corn, green vegetables, fruits, and nuts, and divide the harvest.

D dawa is medicine
(dah·wah)

Africans have always had many nature-cures for illnesses. Certain herbs are used to make a tea for reducing fever; other herbs help cure a stomachache or cold.

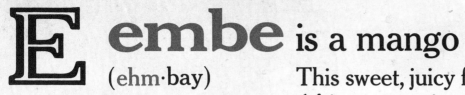

E embe is a mango
(ehm·bay)

This sweet, juicy fruit found along the East African coast is curvy shaped and golden in color. Mangos in other areas are oval or round with green, red, or gold skin.

F fagio means broom
(fah·gee·oh)

Made from long straws tied near one end, brooms are used to sweep the floors of the home and the smooth clay grounds around the homestead.

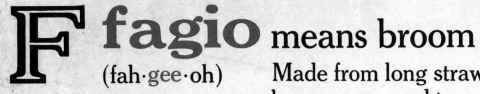

G gudulia is a clay jar

(goo·doo·lee·ah)

Jars of clay are made by a potter. They are used for keeping water for cooking and washing, or for storing grain for the next planting season.

H heshima means respect
(heh·shee·mah)

Children are taught early to show respect for adults and older children. In many communities it is the custom for even grown people to kneel when greeting an older person.

I ibada
(ee·bah·dah)

means worship

Africans worship God in many ways.
The Muslim religion is one of the most
widespread in eastern Africa.

J jambo means hello

(jahm·bow)

The formal way to say it is Hu jambo. With these words the long, courteous greeting begins.

K karibu
(kah·ree·boo)

means welcome

A caller says, Hodi? which means
May I come in? The reply is always
Karibu, whether it is a relative,
friend, or stranger.

L lipo is payment

(lee·po)

At the marketplace goods are sold using coins and paper money. In some markets payment is one item traded for another.

M mama means mother

(mah·mah)

The mother teaches her daughters homemaking skills, like grinding corn, cooking, and making handicrafts. She teaches both daughters and sons to help care for the younger children.

N ngoma
(n·go·mah)

is drum and dance

Ngoma means both drum and dance, as drumming and dancing are commonly done together. Nowadays a party with modern music and dancing is also an ngoma.

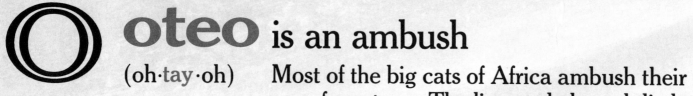

O oteo is an ambush
(oh·tay·oh)

Most of the big cats of Africa ambush their prey from trees. The lion and cheetah lie low in the tall grass and spring upon a grazing zebra or hartebeest.

P punda is a donkey

(poon·dah)

The donkey is an important animal to farmers of some areas. Donkeys transport the harvested crops from the farmlands to the homesteads.

R rafiki is a friend
(rah·fee·key)

Children do more than play with one another. Together friends do chores like tending cattle or fetching water from the river.

S shule
(shoe·lay)

is school

Because the climate is warm, many country schools hold classes outdoors. But in the rainy season the classes must meet inside the school building.

T tembo is the elephant
(tem·bow)

Across the savannah lands elephant herds move in search of food and water. With other animals of the plains they gather around a waterhole to drink and bathe.

U uzuri means beauty

(oo·zoo·ree)

Beauty means different things in different parts of Africa. In one it is a woman with a clean-shaven head; in another it is a great crown of braided hair.

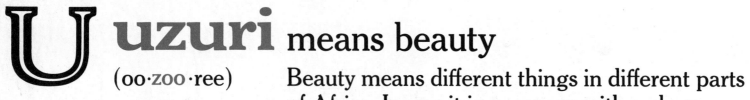

V vyombo are utensils

(vee·oam·bow)

A craftsman makes utensils for the village. Carved wooden bowls and ladles and pitchers made from gourds are useful and decorative objects for the home.

W watoto are children
(wah·toe·toe)

Children play out of doors most of the time. Sometimes they form a circle to play a rhythmic game with funny songs, quick steps, and hand clapping.

Y yungiyungi is a water lily

(yoon·gee·yoon·gee)

These huge pink or white flowers are found floating along the edges of lakes and ponds. In some places the roots are used as food.

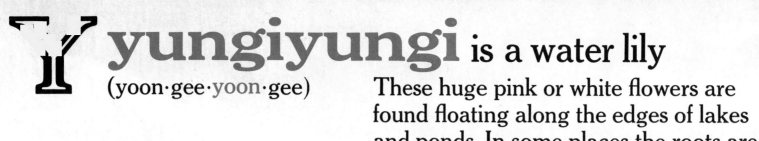

Z **zeze**

(zay·zay)

is a stringed instrument

This musical instrument is the great-grandfather of the banjo and the guitar we know today. The xylophone, too, comes to us from Africa.

MURIEL FEELINGS was born in Philadelphia and went to California State College. She has lived in East Africa, where she taught for two years. Mrs. Feelings now lives in Philadelphia, where she is on the parent council of an independent Black school and works for a Black community service organization. Muriel and Tom Feelings' first book, *Zamani Goes to Market*, received enthusiastic reviews, and their second book, *Moja Means One: Swahili Counting Book*, was a Caldecott Honor Book in 1972.

TOM FEELINGS, well-known artist and illustrator, was born in Brooklyn and attended the School of Visual Arts. Mr. Feelings lived in Ghana for two years and has traveled extensively in East Africa. He is now working with the recently established government publishing program in Guyana, South America, where he is training young artists in textbook illustration.

A NOTE ABOUT THE ART

Tom Feelings prepares his art in several stages. He makes his first drawing and then transfers it onto a rough textured board in pencil, then goes over it with a pen filled with water-soluble black ink. This gives him his base art. Then he paints the areas of the picture that will remain light or highlighted in the final painting with white water-based tempera paint. Next he lays a wet sheet of tissue paper over the complete board, which causes the black ink and the white tempera to run together, creating interesting shapes and forms. While the tissue is still wet, he paints ink washes into the darker areas and more white tempera, sometimes mixed with ink, into the lighter areas or over darker sections. Then the process of rewetting and painting into different sections continues until he feels he has captured the right mood. Finally linseed oil is used to accent some dark areas and bring out parts of the base line drawing.

The final effect is a picture so luminous and so subtle that conventional reproduction becomes impossible if it is to retain the essence of the original work. Although the art is prepared with only black ink, white tempera, and linseed oil, reproducing it in only black and white maintains neither the strength nor the warmth of the original art.

After many different tests were performed by the printer, a final decision was made: to photograph the art in what is called double-dot. Basically this is a technique in which each piece of art is photographed twice. The first shot, which is called the key plate, includes all of the art and is printed in black ink. The second shot includes only portions of the art and is printed in a different color, in this case ochre (see color square below), which was decided upon after additional tests. The second color is not obvious in the final book, but has the effect of enriching the reproduction and maintaining the strength, subtlety, and warmth of the original art.